CW00670266

NEVER
PASS
A GATE

by
Nick Wotton

Forest Publishing

First published 2003 by Forest Publishing
Republished as a revised and enlarged edition in 2004
by Forest Publishing
Woodstock, Liverton, Newton Abbot TQ12 6JJ

Copyright © Nick Wotton 2003 & 2004

All rights reserved. No part of this book may be
reproduced or transmitted in any form or by any means
electronic or mechanical, including photocopying,
recording or by any information storage or retrieval
system, without written permission from the publisher

British Library Cataloguing in Publication Data.

A catalogue record for this book is available from the
British Library.

ISBN: 0-9536852-8-4. 2nd revised and enlarged edition
(ISBN: 0-9536852-6-8. 1st edition)

Designed by Phil Stronach
PO Box 194, Newton Abbot. TQ12 6XG
Tel: 01626 330440

Printed and bound in Great Britain by
Wotton Printers Limited, Newton Abbot, Devon TQ12 4

Forest Publishing

NEVER PASS A GATE

ppose that I was around the age of four when my heart was taken by magic of Dartmoor.

very first recollections of this wonderful area were from the windows he Tor Bus.

as always a real treat for our family to make the pilgrimage to the hills vay of the old bus that left Newton Abbot and wound its way up to ecombe in the Moor through the South Devon countryside. How I ed those journeys and today they are treasured memories from a py childhood spent here in Devon through the late 1950s and 1960s. n recall quite vividly my excitement as - from the top of Widecombe - I stood open mouthed absorbing the views in every direction for the first time. That memory has remained with me to this day, and my s on Dartmoor since have always been so special to me.

great friend and walking companion Bernard came out with a saying day: "Never pass a Gate". These were words passed on by his father, on our many strolls we seldom pass a gate.

hese present times we often find our days full of rushing here and re, with no chance to 'take our breath' and unwind. I hope that if you yourself with this book in your hand, that you will enjoy the simple ds - written from the heart - of a proud Devon lad. And maybe, just be, you will pass fewer Dartmoor gates and see our beautiful land as er before.

hin the covers of this book I have written, there are poems to friends nown to you, but I make no apologies as these ely people have inspired me in so many erent ways and this humble offering is for m.

thanks go to my lovely family, who share me Dartmoor, and of course my great friend 'Bern' makes our walks so enjoyable. Also, many nks to Judy Chard for listening to ideas and encouraging me in this k.

n of course extremely grateful to Kate Van der Kiste and Angie clure for their poems featured in first edition of Never Pass A e. This second edition now sists of all my own verse and I cerely hope that you will enjoy the poems which have been added for revised book.

Nick Wotton

STONE

As winter days get lighter
I'll soon return to my old stone
And spend some time just thinking
In the spring sun, all alone

To many just another stone
On the barren empty moors
But me a place of solitude
To dream amongst the tors

I stand and watch the endless stare
From the face that seldom smiles
Whose fate was set upon this hill
And viewed from countless miles
With rigid features, ice cold eyes
Weathered through the years
Fierce storms so harsh and painful
Create your granite tears
Still you hold such dignity
Amongst dying bracken and wild gorse
No plea for your forgiveness
Only shadows of remorse
The legend says those brazen witches
Put your hunting to an end
Emblazon you in Dartmoor stone
Such a sad and lonely friend

As winter rain clouds, black the sky
Wild gales rip at every tree
Take a glance to Houndtor
At least your hounds run free
From Manaton , a night so bright
I took rest against a stile
The moon shone upon an old grey face
To force a rare wry smile
For as long as I can clamber up
Hayne Down, and to your home
You will always share my sympathy
And never stand alone
I have often sat below your frown
Dark eyes reach across the moor
Searching out an answer
And for the witches curse, a cure

Granite man of Dartmoor
Stuck so fast upon the hill
How I admire your courage
As you face the winter's chill

The Bowerman's
Nose In Winter

The Hairy Hands Of Dartmoor

To drive across the cold grey road
From Princetown, in the night
Take care to keep your windows closed
Make sure the steering wheel's held tight.

For years ago from nowhere
As many a folk will tell
The hairy hands would follow you
And all would not be well.

As winter storms rolled over Dartmoor
The grazing stock would hide
For to travel east to Postbridge
At your peril you would ride.

At the Cherrybrook the water's crossed
By a granite bridge of stone
It would be wise at this strange old spot
Not to dwell alone.

There under the towering tors
That peer down from the moor
Stories tell of hairy hands
From days not long before.

A chilled feeling in the atmosphere
Could fill your car with fear
The wheel you held would tighten
When the bridge became quite near.

Some victims of this experience
Insist the story's real
They all agree that hairy hands
Had gripped their steering wheel.

We shall never know the reason
For this Dartmoor mystery
This phenomenon has ceased it seems
At last the trapped is free.

The Calling Of Jan Coo

Legend tells of poor Jan Coo
Whose freedom, pixies took
He was just a simple labourer
At a farm they call Rowbrook

A happy lad, he worked the land
Above the gorge, where flows the Dart
The river known to Dartmoor folk
Its wild obsession for a heart

One bitter winter evening
To the kitchen, Jan Coo came
To his friends that gathered by the fire
He said: "someone calls my name"

Far deep below the raging Dart
Crashed her angry waters through
Pounding out her fearful cry
The cry was for, Jan Coo

With lanterns gleaming in the dark
A search was carried out
No human voice had called the boy
Of this, there was no doubt

The men climbed up the wooded hill
And made haste for Rowbrook Farm
Securing doors and windows
Keeping warm and safe from harm

Those winter nights were fearful
Dartmoor weather, foul and harsh
The cry for Jan kept calling
From the pit at Langamarsh

The broadstones see the river bend
Its waters scupper by
Echoes speak her appetite
Still the desperate Dart would cry

Springtime brought the lighter nights
It seemed the danger passed
Surely, cries for Jan Coo's heart
From the deep gorge, could not last

But at twilight on a working day
Returned the haunting voice
Jan Coo was summoned to the Dart
He really had no choice

The calling came from Langamarsh Pit
Where they say the pixies dwell
Who had called the poor lad there?
It is hard for folk to tell

As hopelessly he ran to the Dart
Seeking out this mystery
Never to be seen again
Jan Coo's soul could not be free

Who stole this lad from Rowbrook Farm?
To the river through the trees
Was it pixies? Or the hungry Dart?
Or whispers from the Dartmoor breeze?

8

Horsham Farm

...ve where River Bovey
...es her way through Horsham Cleave,
...moor's beauty so abundant
...ire's gentle hand does weave.

...e stands an ancient farmhouse
...ming with such special charm,
...me so full of whisperings
...e comes this tale from Horsham Farm.

...y years have passed us by
...e from the wars, a lad came home,
...kinfolk glad to see him
...his return was not alone.

...from his brave adventure
...ad gained a Spanish wife,
... along with her dear mother
... about to change his life.

The family at this farmhouse
No compassion, would they show,
"Either find these people somewhere else,
Or you my son, must go."

Left with no alternative
And with the ultimatum, his family gave
The desperate lad found a little home
Up in the woodland, in a cave.

The poor boy found retribution
For causing his ladies so much harm,
He met his awful fate one night
By the fireside, at Horsham Farm.

The females left so wretched
Wandered through the eastern moor,
Selling herbs and simples
At any open friendly door.

...ecially for Peter and Hazel Manners-Chapman
...o first told me of this story in the old shippon
at Horsham Farm.

9

Chatting With Ena

Where the lanes meet down in Ponsworthy
The Webbern gains another stream
People stop to view this sight
Of peace and charm serene
I always walk the river path
To reach the cottage on the end
In steps of hope that with luck today
I can speak with a gentle friend
When passing through an old wood gate
I shall often find a smile
And from her doorway Ena steps
To talk with me awhile
We seldom put the world to right
Or discuss matters of the day
Pass some time just chatting
In our well versed Devon way
The folk we know in different parts
Always make our conversation
News of friends or events of note
Or the plight of a close relation
It is just a joy to spend my time
At this cottage whilst on my way
I hope that Ena will be there
When strolling past another day

MY GATE IN AUTUMN

A breath of autumn brushed the trees
And spoke across Lyme Bay
As telling evening shadows
Crept towards a yesterday
Mirrored fields along the Teign
Seen weaving patterns to the downs
Where bracken now so spent and frail
Displays the season's rustic gowns

My gate at which I dwelt a while
A link from moor to sea
For a moment here, I lost myself
With no call to rescue me
As rollers pound the sandstone cliffs
In a dance of anger fraught
My eyes have fixed towards the hills
Never lost to me in thought

The last days of the blackberry feast
Tired hedgerows calling time
Summer whispers fond farewells
A final harvest now is mine
As a taste of autumn's sweet fruit
Will live forever from this day
And my gate will always beckon me
When once again I take this way

Sunset At The Beacon

I clambered up beside the wall that leads to Buckland Beacon
The evening sunshine, slipping slowly from the sky
Away towards the barren hills on fire with blood red dusk
Day falling from my feeble grasp, in June air - clear and dry.
Face still warm from summer sun, mind in comfort mode
Below the Dart was calm and still as for the sea she made
Alone and able through my eyes, I sat with peaceful gaze
With fortune to experience another Dartmoor sunset fade.

Never Pass a Gate

I heard a Devon adage
From a dear old walking mate
Words passed on by his father
He said "never pass a gate"

Those words have seldom left me
The wisdom seems so clear
As I lean upon a Dartmoor gate
Surveying land I hold so dear

It matters not if you are in a rush
Or even if you are late
Trust my friend's old saying
And never ever pass that gate

When the world seems packed with turmoil
Not enough hours to fill the day
Just pause against an old wood gate
And dream it all away

This poem is for you Bern. Thanks for being there.

The Bridge

Never have I ever met
One soul upon this bridge
That spans a friendly river
Where ferns cascade down from a ridge

Warm peace of June's serenity
Summer sun flecks through weeping boughs
Mother Nature's Dartmoor home
Her beauty she endows

Listening to sweet harmony
Of whispering waters passing through
So many days I have rested here
In dreams, my thoughts drift too

I wonder just, how many eyes
Have feasted at this place
Webburn's power of such tranquillity
Brings a smile to any face

Taking time from modern life
The only rushing here
Are the dragonflies that spend their day
In the valley, I hold so dear

The sounds released of peace asleep
Reach not up through the trees
But resound by my old bridge I love
On a gentle Dartmoor breeze

he Devil Calls At Poundsgate

A cruel day in late October
Back in 1638
Storm clouds filled the Dartmoor sky
Above the inn at old Poundsgate

At the door there came a knock
A bedraggled stranger stood
He was hard to recognise
Hid beneath his dripping hood

Outside crashed thunder through the hills
Ferocious rain still teeming
Sat by an open roaring granite hearth
The dark stranger's coat was steaming

A fearful landlady, ill at ease
Brought forth a jar of ale
He thanked her for her kindness
But his presence left her pale

The stranger by the crackling fire
Took a gold purse from his coat
And paid for his refreshment
As it sizzled down his throat

He smiled and showed his horrid teeth
An evil grin for sure
Before he left The Tavistock Inn
To gallop east across the moor

His destination, Widecombe
He rode hard, then even faster
Until he reached the parish church
Where soon would be disaster

At the inn, the locals breathed a sigh
The landlady still aghast with fear
Clasping only leaves in trembling hands
She knew the devil had been here

Shelley

From Dartmoor's streams and rivers
Reflections of sparkling eyes
Clouds you raced on rolling downs
Silhouettes on living skies

On the gentle winds that stirs the gorse
And leans wild heather to and fro
I still watch you weave such cunning tracks
Your curiosity would always show

On days you leapt upon the rocks
Seeking vantage over granite tors
Those moments lazing, in floods of sun
Head lain on tired paws

Curt winter days so bare, so chill
Slicing deep down to our bones
Seeking out those hideaways
Our Dartmoor second homes

Together for your lifetime
Just as long as fate would let
A face that never told me a lie
My mind, refuses to forget

Through these eyes that search a land
We love and roamed so free
Somehow I seek, although apart
Dartmoor brings you back to me

When memory is all we have
How sweet, my thoughts I keep
A dear friend Shelley always was
Not gone, but just asleep

The
Lane

ong the lane from Bonehill rocks
eldom walk too fast
n steps of hope, that maybe
My stroll will always last.

Anger forms in darkening skies
Clouds laden, full of rain
Across the valley, Hameldown
So thrilled I am here again.

Bracken reaching to those tors
Where dreams today are few
Swirling mist shrouds copper downs
Now taken from my view.

Hawthorns bravely stand their ground
Against Dartmoor's fiercest blow
Gorse still clings to barren earth
And will ever bloom and grow.

Below, towards our granite tower
Scattered farmsteads fade
Their hand-tilled land, now little used
Today, only rabbits here have played.

With older eyes that scan this land
The River Webburn carves apart
No wiser me in such troubled times
Still this old track stirs my heart.

So as my life drifts swiftly on
And my verve is getting lower
This lane laced with such peaceful times
I shall walk a little slower.

A Summer Evening
At Mel Tor

I have a single rugged stone
Where a part of me forever lives
A place for me to sit and dream
The dreams that Dartmoor gives

Above the gleaming, busy Dart
Buzzards glide silently above
Solace from the world's clenched fist
This peace I always love

Many days my time I've spent
From Mel Tor looking out
No finer way to view my hills
Of this, there is no doubt

When summer sunshine leaves the moor
Evening shadows grow in length
The power of tranquil Dart gorge
Will always give me inner strength

When the golden sunset slips away
And the first shiver of the night
Alone upon this granite throne
Where wrongs are turned to right

Nature's nightshift starts its day
This evening's glow forlorn
Let's hope for humans peace will reign
Until the new day's born

A Smile from the Woodland

Through the trees you loved so much,
An April sunlight kissed the river.
The breeze that brought such sorry news
Felt raw and caused a shiver.
I sat rapt on the mossy rocks
That cram the Bovey's waters,
With thoughts for family missing you,
Your loving wife and daughters.

The wood seemed rather lonely
Subdued, was birdsong too,
Silent boughs swayed on the trees
How your valley misses you.
A smile that lit so many walks
Not here for me today,
Will always be remembered
Each time I pass this way.

Bluebells start their woodland show
As yet another summer grows,
Brighter days will return to us
Where the Bovey gently flows.
I know that somewhere in these woods
Or when the church bells sound,
The spirit of a lovely man
In every season, will be found.

The sadness that will fill the days
And the emptiness we feel,
Will change in time to memories
As your warmth was truly real.
The days our paths met in the woods
Chatting, passing time
And together sharing humour
The pleasure was indeed all mine.

ADDER

By the scattered bricks of Red Lake's past
As the summer shadows grew
We stumbled on your resting place
As people always seem to do!
We meant no harm to you old friend
Just walking on your moors
Or disturb you in your habitat
Or even wake up 'her indoors'.
But from the anger in your eyes
You left us under no illusion
Visiting your grassy bank
Was for you - a great intrusion.

The lady friend curled up so snug
Failed to wake and see the dangers
From us Dartmoor walkers and a dog
To you just total strangers.
But you followed every move we made
And hissed out your dismay
Protecting every blade of grass
Where Mrs Adder lay.
Such bravery you showed to us
And the courage that it took
Was not in vain old Adder friend
You're now featured in this book.

**Photograph by my good
friend Alan Watson**

20

The Aune in March

Springtime seemed a world away
With few thoughts in my head
Along the Aune I picked a path
The cold clouds, dark as lead
A bitter wind blew from the east
Snapping fiercely at my face
Southern Dartmoor felt so wild today
Yet stunning in her grace
Remains of poor men's industry
Beside the river, are heaped
Fortune promised for toil and graft
Rewards, bare hands seldom reaped
These men of Dartmoor, arms of steel
Kept hunger from their door
Poignant granite monuments
Still lay on this lonely moor
The clapper bridge, I never pass
Dark waters charm my stay
The tempo of the flowing Aune
Will steal an hour from this day
For as the wind that chills me so
Suggests it's time for home
I know that soon I will return
Again these paths, to roam
But for the tinners of the Aune
Again, shall never work the streams
The Aune still full of their sweat and hope
And ghosts from disused beams

Jay's Grave

Tiny grave beside the lane
Facing bravely, winter's chill
Legend states, you were a suicide
From a farm, beneath the eastern hill

If true, you lived a wretched life
In your short time, full of pain
Now sleeping here in dignity
Since James Bryant, built your grave again

Today you lay, a soul at peace
And each and everyday
A short sad life, remembered
By sweet flowers people lay

Never to be forgotten
A grave that Dartmoor tends
The lonely desperate farm girl
Who has now, so many friends

Benjie Tor

Radiant winter sunshine strained my eyes
Magnesium burning from Dartmoor skies
The water at Venford glistening bright
This gift of a day that felt so right

A soft track led me to the edge of the hill
I descended, to avoid the northerly chill
Below bare limbs as the woodland did start
Pointing a way to the rocks on the Dart

Picking a route through the carpet of moss
To the cascading brook and a place I might cross
Then up trodden paths to again reach the moor
And take in the view from my perch at the tor

The bitter wind hitting so hard at my skin
But the sounds of the Dart were warming within
With the constant song of the valley below
A familiar contentment was beginning to grow

Many days I have spent taking time to reflect
At a world where peace seems too much to expect
I will always recall my hours at this tor
Enticing my senses to come back for more

Sharing the thoughts of so many like me
With a wish for wild comfort - a taste to be free
Come Benjie Tor dreams, from the valley below
Reluctant to leave but it is time I should go

EVENING

On Buckland Common evening comes
For the ponies there who graze
A sun so blistering in July
Now benign in western haze

Flame tips of the southern moor
Rise and dance with ochre skies
A Dartmoor sunset once again
Performs before my eyes

Those fields that form a tapestry
Climbing half way to the tors
Merge in shadows, deep and dark
Across these sleepy moors

Amongst the furze and heather
So soon to flood the ground
The rip of ponies at the turf
Is this evening's only sound

Their space I share so silently
Once nervously, they glanced
Now foals feed at this stranger's feet
In whose friendship they have chanced

Alone with just this herd and thoughts
As evening warmth shall drift
Until furtive Dartmoor predators
Fly low to eye their pending shift

But me, I'll taste the evening come
Fading colours muted, calling
The calm forever reaching in
Just before the night stars falling

Ripples of the empty hills
Splaying far out to the west
Sometimes as evening steals a day
These moments often are the best

East Dart In Winter

The new year came to Dartmoor
Welcomed warmly by the snow
A cloudless sky looked down on us
The East Dart in full flow
We left the world at Postbridge
As the wood fires there were burning
To flirt with East Dart's water course
And the hills my heart was yearning
With every footstep tell-tale
Planted in last evening's fall
The landscape was still slumbering
Beneath a sparkling shawl
So often at the waterfall
Where the brave young waters slide
My mind has been revitalised
Letting all my thoughts just glide
Today as warm and cold will vie
To reach deep into my heart
I shall take a stirring memory...
This winter day along the Dart

Dedicated to my friends, Barbara and Roger Beauchamp,
who shared this wonderful day with my son James and I. 25

Storm
Clouds

When storm clouds gather in the west
It is a time I love the best
Great walls of darkness grip the moor
Climb into my coat and close the door.
Down the track, across the burn
The hills open up, through the gates
I need to race as the rain will fall
To a landscape where only nature dictates.

In the distant valley far away
I'll reach the place to pass the day
Just sit in my small rock abode
And watch the lead grey sky explode.
Tears of those who've gone before
Flood the brooks and streams
So snug my granite canopy
Outside the rain still teems .

My senses tell me the worst is past
How I wish this storm would last
I know that every drop is spent
The storm is gone and clouds repent.
Once more the landscape springs to life
Its body cleansed by rain
How I hope, the land I'll taste
And a Dartmoor storm again.

Many thanks to Lucia Bruderer for the use of this stunning photograph

As the Swincombe river meets the Dart
Another life vein from the moor
Across the steps to towering pines
I shall take a rest for sure
Fortune here has favoured me
No other soul to share this place
It is early June and a sultry sun
Spares warming rays upon my face

My mind recalls the many times
These banks have been my seat
Drowning in such total calm
Taking weight off two tired feet
On other days the angry Dart
Would pound her way towards the sea
Dartmoor raging in full rush
With no crossing place for me

But here upon this warm bright day
With all the new life now displayed
My eyelids may well join awhile
By the rivers in the shade

SHADE

Hawthorn

What's this that stands against a wind
Whose fingers chase the sky
An empty frame of brittle songs
Always here to please my eye

Old friend I watched from sheltered combe
As you battled steadfastly
Against the stinging hailstorm
That lashed through you and me

Dreams of clean white blossom
Promise fruit of deepest red
A sanctuary from the summer sun
Where the blackface rests her head

Against gentle hues of autumn
Bracken fading fast to ground
Songs of the Dartmoor hawthorn soothe
Each perfect note now found

When too frail to reach your tor
And only memories left for me
I shall take these days, we stood as one
Watching clouds drift by, so free

Despair of Spring

Dark days follow dark nights
As the light nights open out
The torment of our farmers
Existing in the realm of doubt.
The moor lays calm but helpless
In fear of what might come
To those of us, who care for her
I feel her pain just like a son.

Fighting the compulsion
To roam so free across the land
Giving Dartmoor hope of life
And friends a helping hand.
How I wish that I could aid
In such desperate times for you
I pray soon the nightmare will be quelled
Then your spring will start anew.

When the March wind bites into your face
The moorland air feels clean
Time drifts over lamb-filled fields
As on a wooden gate you lean.
Hedgerows begin to speak again
With a voice so crisp and clear
Only time can heal our farmers' hearts
My thoughts are always here.

How I long for days to come
The problems will be defeated
To sit upon the Tors once more
Where the peace again is greeted.
The terror of this spring I hope
Will leave the Dartmoor farms alone
And I can walk the beautiful hills
My heart tells me, is home.

The outbreak of foot and mouth disease in 2001 was a very bad affair indeed. For me personally it meant that my visits to Dartmoor would have to stop until the disease had gone. My thoughts were for friends who were caught up in the restrictions and were devastated by the results of this awful scourge. It had a profound effect on many businesses and farmers - and with them very much in mind, I wrote my poems Primrose and Despair of Spring.

Primrose

Stark winter days were dark and long
Our spring growth still asleep
Each primrose senses something's wrong
In silent hedgerows, subdued they weep
Natures network spreads the word
Of such problems on its land
I hope that strength of summer rays
Will offer spring a helping hand

High on the hills I miss so much
The lonely days go by
Friends that work this beautiful place
Just wait and wonder why
Hawthorns stand on the empty downs
I have loved for all my years
The primrose once such a joyful friend
For Dartmoor sheds her tears

In the fields few cattle graze
Where the life will start once more
So strange the feeling on the land
All is so unsure
The vibrant Devon countryside
We thought should never die
This tragic year fights hard to live
As sweet primroses still cry

The Lady
By The River

To my dear friend Judy

Across the bridge in the land of streams
A cottage sleeps alone, bursting with dreams
Its borders kissed by the Lemon's flow
With a garden loved by hand and hoe

Through the stable door and enter a heart
Whose passions rise and fall, like waters of the Dart
The love of the man, her critic and friend
Still fills her life and will never end

The kitchen table where we sometimes sit
And our observations of life, together transmit
A changing world, for the worse it seems
But the lady by the river, still smiles and dreams

The world is full of push and shove
The cottage by the river is a place I love
Where the joys of living are always embraced
And its cruel twists of fate, will ever be faced

Really, it is not hard to pretend
How much I enjoy this time to spend
Just sitting in the land of streams
And listening to this lady's dreams

Chirpy

Whenever I'm in Chagford
At any time of year
I seem to meet old Chirpy
At the Buller's drinking beer

How much I enjoy the banter
With this dear old Devon boy
I'd love to spend more time with him
His humour such a joy

I remember one day back along
I was driving down a road
Old Chirpy in his tractor
Was cutting hedges in his Chirpy mode

He stopped and had a chat with me
And asked if I was fine
Not noticing the traffic jam
Stacked behind him in a line

It didn't seem to worry him
As horns began to blow
He would move his tractor only
When he decided he would go

I suppose for all the folk behind
He was just impossible to pass
But to me, he's just old Chirpy
And in a very different class

I really should go back there soon
And in Chagford, time I'll spend
Search out dear old Chirpy
Who is everybody's friend

There have been so many people
In Chagford through the past
But my memories of this friendly man
I am sure will always last

River Dart so serene
As you flow between the tors
A journey to a waiting sea
From your birth upon the moors

The trees stoop down to kiss you
Relentlessly you creep
Through a gorge, where the inhabitants
With your music, gently sleep

I followed nature's signpost
That points from in my heart
To the place I share with dippers
The broadstones on the Dart

Where sable waters cut a path
Beneath the doctor's drive
And a river full of energy
Makes me glad to be alive

Never do you disappoint me
When I feel that I must call
Sit and share your symphony
As you so peacefully enthral

Days when sunlight finds me here
As it rains down from the skies
To see the Dart's real character
I just sit and close my eyes.

The Pipe That Won't Go Out

On the bank of the Becka Brook one day
Winter shadows slipping down from granite tors
For me another walk was soon to end
And a time of peace upon my moors

I climbed the steep and winding path
To Houndtor and the feeling I was free
Stopping just to take some precious time
Then visit Alan's little van for a welcome tea

Like so many other days
I was met by this friendly man
Which is probably the main reason
Why I call here, when I can

His warmth is always there to see
Even when winter's weather is grim
It really is no real surprise
Why so many friends visit him

He is there for you regardless
Of the season or adverse weather
After the winter snow has fallen
Or when the moor is clothed in heather

For many years you have been our friend
Our advisor, doctor, vet
The conversations, moans and laughs
Precious times we'll not forget

I know it's time to take a rest
And enjoy your well earned break
You are a very special man
And deserve the plaudits people make

Bern and I have brought our friends
From so many different places
You have made each one feel so at home
Like people, and not just faces

So when you pack your pipe away
And Houndtor sheds a little tear
The era of a lovely friend ends
In our thoughts, we hold so dear

Tina

Tina Schultze very sadly died in Stuttgart in 2001. The people who were lucky enough to have known Tina will always fondly remember her. We all hope she has now found peace.

I remember so well the day in June
We walked the Dartmoor tracks
Along the East Dart valley
With the hot sun on our backs

A group, from every nation
We strolled for many miles
Our day was full of happiness
Our faces full of smiles

Your eyes were kind and bright
Your words so softly spoken
We had no reason to surmise
Beneath, your heart was broken

At Laughter Tor we rested
And surveyed the moor in summer glory
Not realising that your life
Was, sadly, another story

Away from all this beauty
In a city, filled with fears
It feels so hard to understand
You had shed so many tears

We showed to you our land of peace
Which you embraced with open heart
The Dartmoor hills and river
You loved right from the start

How sad we all feel, now you are gone
I wish we could have shared your pain
Release the hurt inside you
And then taste Dartmoor once again

I remember the words you spoke to me
Whilst walking on the moors
How much you wished you lived in this place ..
A part of Dartmoor is still yours

Redlake

I rest upon the spoilheap
Take time to breathe and sit
And listen to the voices
Of the men who worked the pit.
The hardy crop of local lads
Who toiled for their families' sakes
Seeking out the white clay
Beneath the black peat, at Redlake.
Their railway crept across the moor
With supplies and with these men
A link to an existence
Travelled time and time again.
On wild and windswept southern slopes
Cold rain slaps so hard against the face
They tried to scratch a living
Dartmoor's arms would not embrace.
Now the track lays dormant
Bricks strewn around in heaps
The dream that once was Redlake
Lays still, alone and sleeps.

The Wicket Maiden at Lustleigh

dedicated to Courtney

My anxious skipper helped me
To put our fielders in their places
The old boys in the slips were glad
Relief spread upon their faces.

A ball that shone like a teacher's treat
Was thrust into my hand
Summer sunshine filled the ground
The wicket looking grand.

"Scorers, are you ready?
Right arm over, play!"
Already sweat streamed down my face
Was this to be my day?

My first ball, a mere loosener
As it sped through to the gloves
The second was a "Jaffa"
No opening batsman loves.

"Keep it going", skipper cried
The third ball passed the edge
"We don't need a mid wicket skip!"
So to fourth slip, we moved Reg.

An attempted 'yorker' nearly worked
But the batsman dug it out
A fifth ball smacked against the pads
I thought it worth a shout.

As I strode back to my bowling mark
A little voice said "Nick ...
Spread your fingers on the seam
And aim for his 'off stick'".

Just like a dart the ball flew down
The batsman played too late
With the sound of tumbling timber
I had bowled him through the gate.

A wicket maiden to my name
To start this opening spell
But fortune changes far too soon
A fact I know so well.

At the end of my third over
I'm less keen on playing cricket
Courtney's boys have found their touch
And Reg is now at deep mid wicket.

It doesn't matter where I bowl
Or how the fielders play
We seem to just be fetching balls
With a pole from the River Wrey.

Afterwards we sat and drank
On that splendid summer's day
No one spoke of the wickets we took
Just...... the ones that got away.

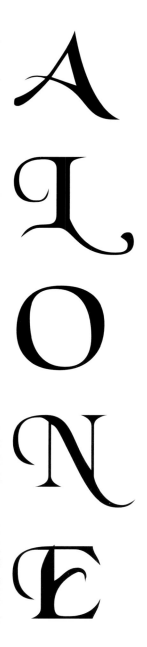

ALONE

The images of any war will always stir up emotions and the 2003 conflict in Iraq has certainly made people take stock of their lives. If anything positive can be drawn from the dreadful pictures we have seen on our screens, maybe it is the realisation that most of us have very little to complain about. I took a short break and looked out over the West Dart River as it snaked its way through the valley at Week Ford and thought just how fortunate I am. I have never taken Dartmoor for granted and in the eyes of the desperate child - Ali Ismaeel Abbas - in Baghdad, I see that these beautiful valleys and hills are even more precious than I thought they were.

In a Baghdad hospital
Alone and scared, in pain
A child the age of my son ..cries
In our quest for Saddam Hussein.
No father has he, to laugh with
No mother to lead him through
No arms has he, now war is here
To wave to me or you.
A caring nurse will help to ease
The burns upon his tiny thighs
She feels each desperate cry for help
With the tears that swell her eyes.
The image of this little boy ..haunts
In our quest for Saddam Hussein
Never will I forget this child
Or at the life I have, complain.

THE FACE OF AN ANGEL

I have often strolled from Southbrook
Past chestnut trees to Buckland Church
Below the tranquil valleys sleep
Filled with holly, oak and birch

Nestling in the hillside there
Bells reaching out to Heaven
No sweeter place to search for peace
Down here in my home Devon

So unique this tiny paradise
It is hard to find another
With William Whitley's gift of time
To remember his dear mother

I shall always stroll from Southbrook
Past chestnut trees to Buckland Church
Below the peace from valleys I love
Speaks through holly, oak and birch

Resting in the Dartmoor ground
A life reaching out to Heaven
So unique this dear friend to us all
In a special part of Devon

Each time that life will take me here
To the clock of my dear mother
I'll recall the smile of Angelene
Never can there be another

Dartmoor Through Tina's Eyes

This poem is dedicated to Tina
Parsons whose lack of mobility
prevents her from fully
exploring the moors, as her heart
would desire.

How I wish I saw Dartmoor's skies
For one day through dear Tina's eyes
The sad fact is reality
That she can't walk the hills with me
The tors that fill her heart with bliss
She would like to stoop and kiss
And the far off hills she yearns so much
I know her fingertips would touch

I will walk the moor for you
Tell of every wondrous view
Show you all the hawthorn trees
That stand so strong against the breeze
Each moorland stream that scuppers by
The buzzards that patrol the sky
The springtime, when the air is clear
Just close your eyes and you are here

Never feel that you are alone
In your head Dartmoor you roam
Look up and see, Houndtor is there
Feel the granite from your chair
The land that fills your loving heart
In your thoughts will never part
When the wild storm over Dartmoor roars
Reach out Tina, this dream's still yours

Thoughts Of September

September sunshine, so tender
I walked my peaceful moor
Thoughts that raced around my head
Were for another shore
Acts of such inhumanity
That filled our eyes with tears
Will darken even Devon's hills
For so many, many years
How I wish the evil winds
That brought you to your knees
Would change its course forever
And blow a kiss upon the breeze
Sad images of such despair
We all fail to understand
I reach across the ocean
To offer you a trembling hand
In sad days sure to test the soul
My heart will feel your screams
The hell on earth you bravely face
Has broken all our hope and dreams

September 11, 2001

A CHRISTMAS BUZZARD

It was a wild and windy Christmas Eve
The sky was stormy, black as coal
No living creature would relish this awful day
Not cattle, sheep, nor foal.
The rust brown hills not barely seen
Alone faced nature's fist
And the granite tors we know so well
    Were hidden in the swirling mist.
        South west gusts blew over me
            As I sheltered from the awesome weather
                Amongst the large grey rugged rocks
                    Caressed with gorse and heather.

Through the valley below my
vantage point
The swollen brook was tracing
Contours of my favourite combe
With angry waters fiercely racing.
From larch trees deep in winter's grip
A friend's call resounded in the air
Then high into the leaden skies
A buzzard's flight my eyes would
share.

Such power of wing, such elegance
She soared and played with ease
Laughing at the Dartmoor storm
That shook and tossed the trees.
    This graceful bird that rose today
        And danced upon my Dartmoor stage
            Gave me the perfect Christmas gift
                To keep for my old age.

Words by Nick Wotton and beautifu
illustrated by Hannah Martin, to who
am so very grateful.

44

Perchance I passed by Corndonford
On a bright and chilly day
The hope that filled my young son's heart
Was meeting ponies on our way
As we approached the old grey farm
Such a warm and genial place
A man with friendly eyes there spoke
With welcome. lined upon his face

My young lad Jack smiled gleefully
As this kind man told my son
That the shires were soon to pull the cart
And he and I could come
Just like their friends and family
We were made to feel at ease
Soon along the lanes we walked
As the wind ran through the trees

What a wonderful experience
Veins of snow still lay uopn the moor
A reminder of the cold wild storm
That battered Dartmoor days before
Spring was fighting hard to prise
Winter's grip from this great land
And a feeling of true horsepower
Flow'd through the reins in Annie's hand

Hail danced over Corndon's slopes
As for home we trotted on
For Jack. part of a special day
With the horses would be gone
But never will he fail to dream
Of his equine friends with charm
Or the warmth of the inhabitants
Shown to him here at this farm

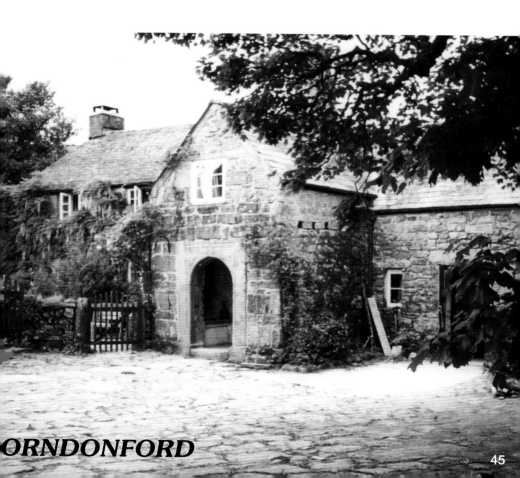

ORNDONFORD

Becky Falls

Sleepy waters leave their birth
Beneath my towering tors
Through muted wooded valleys
Serenely slipping from the moors

Stooping tree boughs, moss-clad rocks
Abundant, lichen grows
Silently the Becka sings
As to the falls, she flows

Her softly spoken voice, so sweet
Nature's words in harmony
This peerless gem of Dartmoor
Where spirits run, alone and free

Suddenly, like tears of joy
Wild emotion from a heart
Bursting through the boulders
Where these wondrous falls will start

I'll find a peaceful nook to dream
Where the russet waters fall
It will always fill a soul with peace
The sounds and sights enthral

As through the Dartmoor seasons
So many varied changes start
A year of diverse beauty
Evolves within this granite heart

Horsham Steps

Dedicated to Brian Moss

Crashing through the maze of rocks
Winter's temper roars,
The foaming veins of Dartmoor's limbs,
Pour down from the moors.
From a heart that pumps a million beats,
The Bovey screams her anger and her pain,
To where the granite boulders lay,
And there they will remain.

Spring brings hope of life to come
As the water's start to ease,
Already in these bright fresh days
Warm sunlight wakes the trees.
The soothing sound of birdsong,
That floats down from the cleave,
This special part of Devon,
My heart will never leave.

To sit upon the giant rocks,
By now just summer's stream,
Will always take my breath away
As in the dancing rays of sun, I dream.
Trout chase shadows in their pools,
Light rays filter down,
Not in these waters will I fall,
But in the peace I'll drown.

Autumn knocks upon the door,
Hazel's garden still parading,
Brown leaves drop from tired trees,
The hold of summer fading.
Down through the wood to Horsham Steps,
On natures path of beech,
How I fear the day will come,
These rocks I'll fail to reach.

47

A visit to Grimspound

I acted as an escort
To a German - rather large
And took him out to Grimspound
For just a pittance of a charge

He seemed to be elated
As he strode along with me
Hungry to explore the place
With all its Dartmoor history

He smiled as I related
All the bumf about the site
Making sure the facts he heard
Were accurate and right

My friend was full of interest
Together as we talked
When our visit was completed
I suggested that we walked

Halfway up the hillside
We paused and turned around
There the Bronze Age ruins
Of the place we call Grimspound

But, I think he'd missed the gist
As he asked me - with straight face
"Did you ever meet a person,
Who had lived here in this place?"

I realised the time I'd spent
Was perhaps for me a waste
Further points of interest
Were now explained to him in haste

My dear old friend from Deutschland
With his gently nodding head
Had spent his day on Dartmoor
Oblivious - to what was said

It was a sultry day one summer
The stifling heat severe
was the leader of a walking group
As normal, chatting at the rear

Somehow I had detached myself
From the others there that day
But up in front a trusted pal
Was heading the right way

I found along beside me
Stride for stride, I had a mate
A rather gorgeous Czech girl
As we reached Stan Fitton's gate

e passed and both his dogs flew out
With their usual greeting here
Stan, from in his garage called
For us to try his home made beer

He didn't have to ask us twice
We accepted in great haste
e beer our friend had brewed himself
No drop of, we would waste

After our refreshment stop
We left and Stan said "cheers"
His hospitality had been first class
And we thanked him for the beers

My friend and I, with faces flushed
Looked fresh and satisfied
The others looked embarrassed
Awkwardness, they couldn't hide

I do believe they thought that we
Had gone and had a ration
something - not like Stan's homebrew
But in a field we'd had some passion

The Czech Girl and Stan's Homebrew

In the garden at The Kestor Inn
My friends seemed quite alarmed
Assuming that their Dartmoor guide
By the Czech girl had been charmed

But I saw suspicion in their eyes
My companion sensed it too
We could not keep the truth from them
And told of Stan's homebrew

Relief soon came to everyone
Because the reason was now clear
Delay was not as they had thought
Just down to Stanley's beer.

ONSLOW

I will never pass your gate, old friend
When my way takes me to you
There is always time that I will spare
And perhaps a carrot too
Your laboured walk across the field
To greet me at your gate
Creates a warmth inside of me
So glad to see you here old mate

The eyes that reach to many hearts
Proclaim just how you feel
With such tenderness you show to all
And your gentle ways appeal
How I savour all our moments
As together two hearts bond
It's always hard to leave you here
For of you I've grown so fond

I'll manage just to drag myself
From this place at which you live
You modestly won't realise
All this pleasure that you give
Old friend I know that very soon
I shall return here to your gate
To spend some precious time once more
With you old equine mate

Dartmoor

e day ever comes when my heart fails to yearn,
 the hills and the valleys I love,
ill be a sign for my soul to resign,
essage for me, from above.
 places I know and the time I have spent,
, one day be all in the past,
the dreams turn into rust and my body to dust,
ay my sweet Dartmoor will last.

If the day ever comes when my heart fails to yearn,
For the rivers that flow from the peat,
Don't tear me apart from the beautiful Dart,
Or the sunlight that plays on the leat.
The memories I hold, are so precious to me,
They are the pot at the rainbow's end,
But forever they are not, in our good makers plot,
And maybe my new life's pretend.

If the day ever comes when my heart fails to yearn,
As the blossom of gorse fills the breeze,
Touching the very instincts that lead me back for more,
Or the wind as it sings through the trees.
The days when the buzzards fly under the tors,
And the black sky fills up with rain,
When I can't recall all these pleasures of mine,
Then Dartmoor won't need me again.

51

Acknowledgements

I would like to thank you, the reader, for taking time to re
my first book. It has given me such great enjoyment writir
Never Pass A Gate
and seeing my work in print is such a thrill.
So many people have been involved in producing this book
and I would like to thank them all for their time and effort
Publisher Mike Lang, who gave me the chance to share m
love of Dartmoor with a larger audience.
My friend Phil Stronach - who has spent so much of his tin
designing and advising me - also deserves my sincere than
Without these people, my poems would still be at the bottc
of a drawer or in the pocket of a coat.
The input of my friends from around the world cannot gc
without a mention; their obvious pleasure of walking on
Dartmoor gives me a great deal of satisfaction.
I must thank TIS for giving me the opportunity of showin⟨
them our part of England.
I am also grateful to other contributors for the use of thei
photographs: Alan Watson for *Adder*, Barbara Beauchamp f
The Aune in March, and Lucia Bruderer for *Storm Clouds*. I
thanks also go out to the characters featured in verse.

Don't forget ... Never Pass a Gate

Nick Wott